GLIMPSE

poems by

Maura Snell

Finishing Line Press
Georgetown, Kentucky

GLIMPSE

ACKNOWLEDGMENTS

Grateful acknowledgments to the following literary journals where some of
the poems in this book have been published:

"The Day She Stopped Telling Me Everything;" "Going to Meet Her, After
Nineteen Years;" "Risk;" and "After She Tells You" appeared in the anthology
Lullabies and Confessions: Poetic Explorations of Parenting Across the Lifespan
(University Professors Press)
"Learning" first appeared in *Mom Egg Review* (MER)
"Dog" first appeared the anthology *Our Last Walk: Remembering and
Grieving our Pets* (University Professors Press).
"Photograph" first appeared in *Brain Child Magazine*
"May" first appeared in *Red Paint Hill Quarterly*

Publisher: Leah Huete de Maines
Editor: Christen Kincaid
Cover Art: *Rise* by Chelsea Bradway
Author Photo: Brenna Snell
Cover Design: Elizabeth Maines McCleavy

Order online: www.finishinglinepress.com
also available on amazon.com

Author inquiries and mail orders:
Finishing Line Press
PO Box 1626
Georgetown, Kentucky 40324
USA

Contents

For my girls—
that includes you, Riley

PHOTOGRAPH

Hey, you, in your tutu,
      tulle-decked and plump

with pots of geraniums
      leaf-licked and blooming about you—

hey, you, there, squat on the cement step,
      fingers wrapped in fists, bare toes wriggling,

where did you go little girl?

You surged,   opening
      the way a new bud might
               when placed in water and sunlight
               in a fast-frame unfurling.

Will you remember when we are dust?

I can feel how the concrete must have
      made your bare skin itch,

      the leotard, thin against your bottom
            pressed down into rough cement,

already a eulogy.

      You've disappeared into gawk and glasses.

But sometimes, when you're not looking,

I squint at you
      and can still see in your profile

      that baby girl,

gazing up at me as she squats

among the geraniums.

CHILD

On Tuesday the child came from me
birthed not as a tiny newborn but as a three-year-old—
wet and hot and slick with amniotic fluid,
arms and legs long and thin and awkward.
This foal-child struggled to stand and stretch
and reached for my breasts heavy with colostrum.

On Thursday, they came out as puppies—
three or four of them—
curling black balls of damp fur pressed
with meconium stain,
wriggling and squirming on a white mat
spread across the foot of my bed.

I felt relief—that instead
of giving birth to a squalling infant
intent upon my constant care
the puppies would survive in a box on the floor
in the corner of my kitchen under a heat lamp
with bowls of warm milk.

SEPTEMBER TWELFTH

Before yesterday, we were all virgins.
Today the sky is silent.
Cumulous clouds act as if nothing is wrong.

We lay in the grass and I watch a breeze
kiss and lift tendrils up off my baby girls' head.

The dogs lay in the shade of the maple tree, unconscious.
I think Stephen Hawking is right.

Hugging the earth
I feel it slow
and I pull my daughter to me
trying to remember the laws of quantum physics.

Before yesterday, my life was a series of history lessons.
Before yesterday those things happened—but not here.

Lady bugs crawl. Dogs sleep. Winds blow. And somewhere
in this space and time continuum,
where planes are grounded and people
are still buried alive under rubble,
my daughter's hand finds my face, press my cheek.

Fat fingers, still sticky with pancake syrup, poke me.

WISH

She says
I hate how I look.

I say
you are made of stars .

I wrap my arms
around her body

and my body
breathes her in

returns her body
to its first home

for safe-keeping
or repair.

Pour I say to my blood
seep into all of her broken places.

She is taller than me now
but still she rests her chin beneath mine.

(Our skin)

And I know even if I could
keep her infant and cradled in my arms,

even if I could
keep her eyes deep with childhood—

all this still
would not be forgotten.

Who is the patron saint of sorrow?
Who is the patron saint of now?

AFTER SHE TELLS YOU

she thinks of killing herself
you are frozen, unable to reach her.
She is this other-species—a woman-child—

who used to sit pig-tailed
and covered in pancake syrup in your kitchen.

The doctor's office is both tomb and haven,
her blue eyes, mask and mirror.

> They remind you of corn flowers
> behind your mother's house
> those afternoons when you'd run through grass—
> you remember all of those jumpers you wore, hand-stitched,
> each a memory in itself—and how you'd fill your arms
> with wild flowers, the weeds stinging, and how the blooms
> would never last, be half-dead by the time you made it
> home. And how your feet could take you

> anywhere.

And here you are—and she lays beside you,

your daughter,

and the air is whistling.

> *It's all right,* you say,

> *I used to dream of disappearing too.*

LEARNING

My daughter hooks a left onto route 30
and forgets to accelerate into the turn
then stutters into the flow of traffic
a little too much.

I remind myself to look at the sky.

My mother never took me out
when I was learning to drive.
It was dad who braved the passenger seat
of the '76 Chevy Malibu,
back when seatbelts
weren't always there, back when
cars were sofas wrapped in sheet metal
and held together with duct tape,
big enough for legs to sprawl in the backseat.

Of course I took you driving she says when I accuse her.

But I don't remember.
Why do our minds play games like that?
Why can't I recall her there in the passenger seat?
She must have gripped the door handle, must have
cursed under her breath as I shifted out
into the whirl. I mean, how did I become
my mother, invisible and perched,
looking up at the horizon?

THE DAY SHE STOPPED TELLING ME EVERYTHING

It wasn't so much the text itself or the pictures attached
that alerted me to this new era in our mother-daughter existence—
no, it was more that I didn't get the news from my child
but from a friend—
and when I called to congratulate my daughter on her achievement
she didn't even pick up her phone.

It occurred to me that
the day she stopped telling me everything
had already come and gone

like the popcorn guy at a Red Sox game,
or the collection basket at Sunday services:
you have to really pay attention or it goes right by
and then, you're left sitting there
on the edge of your seat with five dollars
clutched in your fist.

DOG

I know you by your breathing, the scuffle of your ins and outs.
I know you by your potato sack weight.
In April when the first of the daffodils
brighten the wintered ground

you become a shape-shifter.

In the first week after your death, you are the jogger on the path
in the woods behind our house.
I can tell by your gait.
I wait on the porch as you go by in case you stop for water.

I leave your bowl out on the stoop.

In the second week after your death you are the check-out girl at
Stop-n-Shop.
You smile and hand me my change.
Your collar is clean, your hair shines, your nails polished.
You loved your brushings so I appreciate your perfume.

Do you remember the day you arrived?

We walked together up to the field.
You pulled hard on the leash. It was spring then, too.
The grasses were greening, coming alive under cold.
I let you run from fence post to fence post.

You chased sunlight and mist.

In the third week after your death, you are the commuter train.
You rumble by hourly. I revel in your ever-calm timeliness,
the way you keep safe all the souls you carry. Not once do you veer
from your course to chase a squirrel or rabbit. I am so proud.

Now you are the rain.

You tap dance through the garden shocked with color.
It's all subterfuge—you will not come inside.
I hear your nails click on the stones,
your soft moan, your recalcitrant sigh.

I leave the door ajar.

LEAVING

She is a cliff crumbling into sea.
Spray and salt stick to her cheeks speckled with eyeliner.
She tells her stories, her voice
a needle on vinyl.

The music clicks and scrapes familiar.

She is fading as she manipulates her walker into the kitchen.
This is time's rudest remark.

She casts off her sanity, and it gives way
to her younger self of sixty years ago—
the house in Woodlawn
her father's viola, Irish linen on tables.

I know she doesn't know me anymore.

I know this is the last time.

Outside the autumn sky is sharp with light.
I turn, wave to a shadow fused in the window
even though I am not at all sure
it's still her.

GOING TO MEET HER, AFTER NINETEEN YEARS

We hold hands the whole way there.
You steer with your left palm and knee.

> We've been coming towards this
> for seven thousand days.

> > I've counted them all.

Once, I dreamt of a little girl in the back seat,
    (buckled in tight)

> honey tendrils flying.

> > Pink lips.

> > > Laughter.

Almost there.
    You stop the car
    so I can step out, catch my breath.

Gravel by the road fills my sandals.
When I shake out stones,   one is turquoise.

> I slide it into my pocket.

I wonder
    if she will have my freckles.

I already know
    she has your eyes.

AT MY NEPHEW'S BAPTISM

my sister wears a soft pink muumuu
sequined in smoke.
I hold my nephew as they recite sacred words.

Everyone smiles.

Afterwards we stand on the lawn and eat cake.
The men huddle around phones checking the score.

The women laugh, open-mouthed.
And everywhere there is wind and leaves and late autumn sun.
I sit on the bench tucked under the glowing maple

and hold my nephew. His body
is pliable and reliant, his skin
startlingly new. And the leaves

jump from the ground into the air in one gust,

swirl, hover, float as if to say—

Now. Now. Now.

GLIMPSE

In 1967 my mother died
while giving birth to my older sister.
My sister was a large baby—nearly ten pounds—
and my mother, a small woman, hemorrhaged to death.

The doctors covered my mother with a sheet,
left her body on the gurney as they brought
the screaming, wriggling infant to my father
waiting down the hall.

I have often wondered what it was like
in that place where my mother was—
a high, even hollow of light and lucidity,
a place with no cold or shadows, a place

with only ethereal brightness and utter calm.
My mother says she could see everything—
the world as it lay if she wanted—could see
into the waiting area, could hear exactly what

the doctors and nurses were saying,
and the distinct syncopated *beep beep beep*
of every monitor on every heart
in the maternity ward.

She could see out and above and through
and knew, as clearly and as certainly
that she knew she was dead—
that her husband and daughter would be just fine.

Years later, she would tell us,
her seven subsequent children,
of how she stared down at her body with disdain,
as if it was a well-worn cocktail dress after a party,

crumpled, blemished, diminished.
She would tell us she felt only peace.
Expansive joy. Encompassing love.
And it was only a glimpse.

Every time she tells us the story,
it's the same.
And she always finishes with
I did not want to come back.

I STARTED THIS ONE BUSINESS THAT MUTES THE WORLD
after Matthew Svalinas

I know it sounds strange and uncanny, but we send these tiny
microbes out—wobbly orbs of gel and plastique that are colored any
way you'd like. The mothers in your neighborhood have already
come calling.

They want to swab their ears with our orbs and sit in blissful silence
as children and televisions and dogs bark and bray and call. They
want to sip their muddied coffee in peace.

The fathers are perturbed. The children are perplexed. Who will
listen to them now? I have no idea about accounting.

Despite the conversations at the end of the day mothers still call and
text and email. They want to know about our next
and newer model; if we can develop one that might be
undetectable to human eyes.
Our lab is working on it.

The developers in the Development Department skew the algorithms
with mustard. They scrape the edges and add daffodil paste to fuse
the echoes. They watch cartoons in hopes of gaining answers.

We are still projecting we'll have it by second quarter next year.

BYWAYS

I.

Pushing my hand
into her abdomen
she implores me—
feel.

The soft tissue of her lines
tell me nothing.

I'm not a doctor, I say.

Instead I pour coffee.
Instead I open the blinds.
May sun cascades in—
a lemon drop spotlight.

Dust fairies plié, pulling me
into the dance.

*I'm not
a ballerina either.*

II.

It's as if
she's evaporated—

in one moment
went from flesh
to icy vapor.

I sit by her bed,
talk about nothing,
make chicken soup,
read her the news.

I press friendship
onto her.

I never told her
of that one winter afternoon
in the days after her surgery

when we met—
her husband and I—

on the sidewalk
in front of the market.

He said, *I don't know
if she'll make it.*

I remember how
he shifted
as he spoke,

and the glint,
how he went
from blurred

to crystal,

as if all along I had been
looking at him
through a phoropter

and in one click

all of his hazy lines
sharpened to edges.

It was then I knew
all her secrets.

III.

When her anger registered
I felt yanked from behind,

I wanted to hang up,
but I was afraid
she would never
call back.

I should have known—
instead I took it all in,
swallowed her misery
like sour milk.

Weeks later, when
she lost her hair
she called someone else
to shave off her graying blonde curls

and left me to find her
the next day

with a stocking cap pulled
low over her naked skull.

At night
I drive by and study her house
in the dark

and the absence
of even

a single
flickering
light.

IV.

This morning
I watched the water
in the birdbath
freeze.

In one moment—
blue sky, clear,
reflected in the small pool.
In the next—

gray shuddered, cold.

V.

When I see her now
I pretend
to go about my business.

My voice might
get a little louder,
a little brighter,
a little forced,

because I'm
convincing myself
that the story I'm telling is so much funnier
or deeper, or more relevant

then what it really is.

I pretend
not to see her,

turn my back slightly
away

so she can't make out

the dip of my chin

when I look down to compose myself,
control the urge to wipe my eyes,

to rub the stress lines from my brow.

I pretend she's not there,
that she never was,

that it doesn't matter.

She is not healing;

neither am I.

All we do

is flinch

and look away.

ANGELA ON THE RACK

Somewhere on the swimsuit rack is Angela.

Angela—in her blue and purple striped bikini with
yellow piping sitting on her soft poplin blanket
spread right at the waters' edge—Angela.

I can see her leaning over *People* magazine
pushing her Jackie-O inspired sunglasses off the bridge
of her nose—

Angela.

Will the memory of her sitting there effortlessly splayed

always be there, behind my eyes?

It has been years, but still, I compare.

In a swimsuit, I hide behind reams of design-blasted print—
anything to distract the viewer from what the suit is covering.

And still, there is Angela.

Angela in her bathing suit.

Angela at the edge of the water.

Unapologetic.

Angela.

MAY

With wind blowing across her bare head
resting on the window's edge,

eyes closed,
she dozes. Lines slip from her brow—

massaged away by spring's warm air—
like sunlight, nearly tastable,

lemons in the grass.
We drive slow over smooth roads in muffled

silence.
She has only a few more days.

When we go back, she asks for pizza
which I feed her and she savors that first hot bite,

the tip of the slice sliding down the inside
of her mouth.

I can almost taste the tomato on her tongue.
I tell her it is sweet and ripe and delicate.

She smiles in wan appreciation
and vomits.

After she is gone, I can see her floating
above her shucked shell:

a wince of light,

lemons, fresh tomato

and long drives in spring sun with the windows rolled down.

DEAD SQUIRREL ON MORNING WALK

I pull the dog away from the
tiny corpse split open—
fur matted with road dirt and tire
pops against pavement gray.
Chestnut, charcoal, cream, red.

       I skirt the scene
       as if turning away erases existence.

The dog strains against the leash.
Tomorrow I'll take another route
or trade sides of the street. Avoidance
is key—eyes up from the drying,
the fading, the flies. By next week
it will be done. Pavement
will reappear from under the vermin—
only the slightest of staining.
End of summer, nothing but gravel and road.

RISK

She let them fall asleep together after prom
on the couch in the family room—her daughter, still
dressed in satin and her date still

with his jacket on.
Looking in on them, all she can think is that
they are so small. She marvels

that they both can fit
on the long side of the sectional—
her back to his front,

her chin tucked down
into her chest in sleep.

She steps away and wonders if this is how it will always be—
will she always feel like a bad mother
because she let them stay there at three in the morning,

didn't usher her daughter off to her own bed,
didn't shoo the boyfriend out the door home—
but instead sleeps so well herself,

for once believing
in all that lay in the crook
of that boy's arm.

WORK IN PROGRESS

You curl your hair in the bathroom mirror,
swipe your lips with red.

I say *you're beautiful*
but you don't believe me.
Instead, you cook pasta. Instead
I set the table. As we eat

you make us laugh,
pretending.

Sometimes when I let my mind wander
I imagine we are both seven.
What kind of friends would we be?
How is it fair that I get to know you

in all these ways
but you only know me as this?

I recall my own mother, reflected
in the window above the kitchen sink.
Her eyes, always cast down.
I'd watch, but she'd never look up.

Tomorrow
I'll drive you to the airport,

sit in the car and watch as you navigate the fray,
and I'll only pull away
after you've disappeared under the sign
marked *Departures*.

EARLY AUTUMN

From here I can see
three hummingbirds flitting
among the orange jewelweed

      (spotted touch-me-nots)—

darting and hushed and hovering,
long bills dipping
down and into—

      frenetic and alive.

Whispers of magic—
as if catching sight of them is a glimpse
into some Avalon, some

      plain of honey.

The collective noun for hummingbirds
is charm, or glimmer, or bouquet—
as if we could gather them all to us like

      daughters.

ELEGY

Last night I pulled myself
out of the bathroom window
crept up onto the top of the porch
in three feet of snow
at eleven o'clock at night,

pulled myself
onto the roof of the house
and was syphoned up in deep scarlet blackness
sucked

like snowflakes drifting
sucked
like ash and timber,
I flung red roping around the chimney,
and me, standing there on the peak

braced, I shoveled
because the roof was caving in.

Then, last night, at three in the morning,
I woke to see my nine-year-old hovering by my bedside,
red hair bursting from her head,
crying.

Dreams and nightmares she said.
And I asked her, *what is your home like?*
and she said *cinnamon and strawberries and dog.*
Breathe, I said, kissed her on her freckled forehead.

And I shoveled.

The roof guy, short, muscled, with a million years in the business
sees no trouble with the old roof tiles

but I am afraid of the snow.

Maura Snell was born in New York, and has lived in Colorado, Ohio, Wisconsin, Massachusetts, and now calls Vermont her home. She holds an MFA in Writing from Bennington Writing Seminars, served as poetry editor at *The Tishman Review*, and works as a Legal Assistant in an "outpost" office of a large law firm. She reads and writes poetry whenever she can find the time – her favorite authors right now include Lisa Krueger, Didi Jackson, Lauren Davis, and Meaghan Quinn. Maura is most inspired by the quiet moments of grace in life, like that first sip of fresh hot coffee, that kiss of frost on the window on an October morning, the sound of laughter coming from the kitchen when her daughters come for a visit, or when a firefly alights on the window screen on a summer night. When she's not working, writing, reading, or sleeping, Maura can usually be found on a hiking trail with her husband and two dogs.

www.ingramcontent.com/pod-product-compliance
Lightning Source LLC
Chambersburg PA
CBHW022056080426
42734CB00009B/1365